McDonald

CUSTOM CARS

of the

1950s

THE SKY

**Pictorial History with Original 1950s
Photography of Trendsetting Cars and the Custom Cars Scene**

Andy Southard and Tony Thacker

Motorbooks International
Publishers & Wholesalers

First published in 1993 by
Motorbooks International
Publishers & Wholesalers,
PO Box 2, 729 Prospect Avenue,
Osceola, WI 54020 USA

Motorbooks International books
are also available at discounts in
bulk quantity for industrial or
sales-promotional use. For details
write to Special Sales Manager at
the Publisher's address

Library of Congress Cataloging-in-
Publication Data

Thacker, Tony.
    Custom cars of the 1950s /
Tony Thacker, Andy Southard, Jr.
      p.   cm.
    Includes index.
    ISBN 0-87938-772-6
    1. Automobiles—United
States—Customizing.
2. Automobiles—United States—
Decoration. 3. Photography of
automobiles. I. Southard, Andy.
II. Title.
    TL154.T43   1993
    629.222'0973'09045—dc20
                           93-8137

Printed in Hong Kong

On the front cover: Clif Inman
stands with his low-slung '57
Chrysler, which was chopped
3 1/2in all around by the Wilhelm
Custom Shop in San Jose,
California.

On the frontispiece: Being single,
I ate at Mel's Drive-In often during
the late-1950s and 1960s. It was
one day in 1956 when I pulled up
and photographed this '50 Ford
two-door across the hood of my
new '56 Ford Victoria and through
the drive-in.

On the title page: I took this
overall shot of Mel's in August
1955. Planning a timed exposure,
I'd asked Bob Walls to drive my
T-Bird through the parking lot and
to stop by the corner. To prevent
the tell-tale light streaks of cars
going by I'd put my hand over the
lens to prevent them registering.
Located on the south side of
Salinas, Mel's was the place to see
and be seen. Sadly, it was torn
down in 1973.

On the contents page: Model
Nancy Davis poses on the hood
of Harry Costas chopped and
channeled '41 Ford, which was an
Oakland Roadster Show award
winner.

On the back cover: Lowell "Moe"
Miler of San Jose, California, built
this unique '41 Ford convertible
with its '48 Ford hood and front
fenders, '48 Caddy grille, and '49
Plymouth bumpers. The engine
was a 239ci Mercury flathead.
Inset: Andy Southard is on the
opposite end of the camera in this
shot as he applies paint with a
steady hand.

Contents

Dedication: Remember When   6

Acknowledgments   7

Introduction   8

Custom Cars of the Fifties   14

Index   128

Dedication

*To Patty Southard, my wife and a custom car fan,
in thanks for all the support she has given me over the years.
The following, written by Patty, is one of her favorite poems.*

Remember When

The pink and black poodle skirts, the girls with pony tails,
Dragging Main on Friday nights, and ending up at Mel's.
The Wurlitzer juke boxes were always aglow with lights and sound,
The local skating rink was the most popular place in town.
When all the guys decided their cars should have a name,
and Hollywood Boulevard was truly a walk of fame.
When pin striping was done free hand, not with a wheel,
chicken croquettes at the diner was really your favorite meal.
When you built your first rod you did it all with your two hands,
you drove it proudly, it was not hauled in trucks and vans.
When you could understand the words of a rock and roll song,
let me tell you those days are really long gone.
When drug stores had soda fountains, you could get a cherry Coke,
    or a piece of apple pie,
parking on Main Street Saturday nights just to watch the people go by.
Driving around Christmas Eve just to see everyone's decorations,
making home-made ice cream Sunday afternoons
    for friends and relations.
I could keep remembering back forever, but now it must come to an end,
"See you later alligator," you will hear from me again.

*Patty Southard
August 4, 1989
Salinas, California*

*A ndy Southard, bundled up to
fight off the East Coast winter,
in the early days before he
relocated to California.*

Acknowledgements

Even though Andy had more than enough photographs—his collection spans forty years and contains over 12,000 color slides and 65,000 black and whites—there are contributors to thank. Namely, the people who made it all possible especially the guys that inspired him in the early days: Johnny Clegg, Willie Wilde, Fritz Doering, Bill Acker, and later on the idols who became friends: George Barris, Bill Cushenberry, Dean Jeffries, Larry Watson, Joe Wilhelm, and so many more.

A special thanks goes from Andy to Dave Marasco for 15 wonderful years with the Bay Area Roadster Club.

Thanks must also go to Motorbooks International for agreeing to publish and to the staff there for their cooperation.

Finally, thanks to our respective significant others, Patty Southard and Kathy Berghoff for their loving support and contributions.

I visited California with a friend in 1952, and while cruising around the Los Angeles area we stopped in Pasadena for some food. As we came out we saw Alan Fairbanks getting into his chopped '41 Ford with a Carson top. Alan posed just long enough for me to get two photographs.

Introduction

Here's one photograph I didn't take. It's my '40 Merc at the Oceanside High School parking lot. Sorry about the quality but it's all I have.

Oceanside, Long Island, N.Y., a young Andrew Suydam Southard, Jr., was an enthusiastic participant in the spaghetti feeds held each weekend over at Johnny Clegg's house. And with the lowered Merc coupe and convertibles and channeled Deuces that cluttered the front lawn and driveway, what choice did a guy have but to dig cars? Moonlight self-taught driver training courses in the family's maroon, wide white-walled '40 Olds four-door forced Andy to play dumb when his mother finally got around to giving him driving lessons. The lessons did prepare him for that first car though, and the next step, financing, was arranged through busboy duties at a local barbecue restaurant combined with occasional stable boy income.

The two jobs netted a savings of $250, and through a newspaper ad resulted in the ownership of a shiny '40 Mercury coupe. In that neighborhood no car could stay stock for long, so a set of Belond headers, a Harmon-Collins dual-point ignition and a set of custom seat covers (designed to zap you the instant you grabbed the door handle) took care of that minor problem.

Needless to say it provided pretty good transportation to high school. While there, Andy decided to join the photo club; an innocent move that was to affect his whole life. He liked what he saw and heard so much that he decided to make it his career. Instead of college, the post-high-school years were spent at the New York Institute of Photography in Manhattan. While there, his car tastes gravitated to later stuff and with the $100 profit from the sale of the Merc, a '49 Ford Club Coupe was purchased. Lots of chrome acorn nuts, blue-dot taillights, and two NHRA decals made it stand out for the time being.

Graduation from photography school brought a turning point. A 1952 California vacation was planned. "Billy Acker and myself drove out in a '49 Ford Club Coupe to visit California and to see the weather, the scenery, the cars, and the girls—not necessarily in that order.

"It took four days to drive out west and when we arrived we stayed at Sherry's Motel in Hollywood—it's part of the freeway now. We got to visit Barris Kustoms, Bell Auto Parts, Bob's Drive-In and the Motorama at the Pan-Pacific Auditorium—promoted by Petersen Publishing."

The cars, combined with the weather, the scenery, and the girls, convinced Andy that someday he would become a Californian.

After returning to New York, Andy soon had the '49 transformed into a mild custom with the addition of nosing and decking, frenched headlights, an Olds grille bar, metallic green paint and to top the whole thing off, "gennie" Los Angeles license plate frames.

Several job interviews with prominent photographers followed, but the Korean conflict was in full swing and Andy was now of prime draft age. Just as sure as taxes, Uncle Sam sent greetings and Andy spent the next two years driving officers around the German countryside.

After service duty was fulfilled, California called and a brand new bright red '55 T-Bird (which Andy had fallen for at the Munich auto show) was loaded up and pointed towards the sunset with the intention of attending Brooks Institute of Photography, for the Motion Picture course. Not pleased to discover that there was a nine month wait before he could enroll, Andy went to visit his old buddy "Willie" Wilde who had also gotten out of the service and was living in the central California town of Salinas.

Andy arrived during "Big Week" Rodeo celebration (still a big event in Salinas) and had never seen anything like it. He soon found out that Salinas was also home to plenty of custom car and hot rod action—they even had their own drag strip—to which people came from all over California. The strip operated every third Sunday of the month and Andy and Willie went regularly, especially when the San Paulo brothers were racing their hot '31 Ford roadster sponsored by the "Drive N' Eat" restaurants.

After the drags, it was a custom to "drag" Main, as it was called. Traveling about 20 mph, everybody sat real low in their cars, "being cool" until they eventually arrived at Mel's.

As Andy tells it, "Mel's was located on the south end of town on Main Street. A couple of blocks further south the lettuce fields started and stretched as far as the eye could see. But, Saturday night was the night to drag Main. It was a ritual. One would start in the center of town, drive past the Fox movie theater and head south waving to friends and beeping your horn at pretty girls. At the end of the second block, coming up to the El Rey movie theater, maybe you'd throw in the clutch and blast out with your Smitty mufflers. Seems like you always wanted attention but you didn't want the cops to stop you for loud mufflers—which the Salinas cops were notorious for. The law also stated that no portion of your vehicle shall be lower that the lowest portion of the wheel rim. In those days, it was hard to find a lowered car that was legal.

"As you traveled further south on Main, you would pass the high school where there was always something going on. Just south of the high school on the opposite side of the street was Foster Freeze. Occasionally, there would be some rods or customs parked in the side lot, it being fashionable to sit there and watch the parade.

"Finally, the grand entrance was made into Mel's. We would turn in on Hawthorne Street, cruise through Mel's and see who was there and what was happening. When it was time to leave, we'd head north and turn onto Alisal Street and hit Sal's Drive-In. After Sal's we went up the street to Shelton's, a low-key drive-in, before heading back to Mel's. Usually, we went back the same route, cruising through Sal's once again and down Main Street.

"Dragging Main, Mel's, and cruising were the big things to do and sometimes we'd do it five or six times a night. Looking back at movie film that I have of Mel's and the gas station that was next to it, gas was only

On our list of "must sees" during that first trip to California in 1952 was Barris' Kustom Shop on Atlantic Avenue in Lynwood, California. It was quiet because everybody was probably over at the Pan-Pacific.

thirty-three cents a gallon. And that was for high-test at a Flying 'A' station."

Andy liked it so much, he stayed. Sadly, the job in the motion picture industry failed to materialize and Andy did odd jobs around Salinas. He also looked out for a roadster. Most of the cars were out of Andy's price range but finally he heard through the grapevine of a basket case '27 roadster pickup for sale. After collecting the pieces that were scattered all over the garage he plunked down $400 and dragged it all home.

Quickly, the T became his primary means of transportation, "Who needed a new T-Bird when you had a neat flathead-powered, non-fendered 'T' to drive?"

Drive it he did too. His travels included a 130-mile return trip from the drags one night in a rainstorm without a top or windshield wipers, and occasional drag races with the local Power-Pak '55 Chevy out on Blanco Road.

The only down time after completion was to change the as-purchased canary yellow paint to match the Glade Green Metallic of a newly purchased '56 Ford Fairlane hardtop. With bright red wheels, grille, and firewall, and wide whitewalls, it really stood out.

Andy entered the Street Roadster class at the Monterey Kar Kapades sponsored by the Slo-Pokes, Inc., in March of 1956 and netted a third place trophy and the beginnings of a new career.

Dean Jeffries, one of the finest and most famous pinstripers of the day, was working his magic on cars at the show. Since striping was the trick paint of the era, Andy became intrigued and spent most of the show watching "Jeff." He went home and began practicing. In a matter of a year or so, he was able to stripe well enough to charge for it. Soon, however, lack of steady employment opportunities in the Salinas area convinced Andy to return to New York. Not wanting to tow a car all that way, Andy drove the roadster to L.A. and sold it to a man in Anaheim as a gift for his son. Andy hasn't seen or heard of the car since.

When he arrived in New York in his '56, complete with rake, lakes plugs, 114 hood louvers, pinstriping, and California license plates, Andy created quite a stir among the local rodders and customizers. They all wanted stripe jobs of their own, and since jobs were scarce, Andy and a friend stepped out, and a business was born. That buddy, Kenny

An ad for the 3rd Annual Motorama as it appeared in the September 1952 edition of *Hot Rod* magazine. Sadly, the Pan-Pacific, one of the world's best examples of Streamline Moderne architecture has been razed in the name of progress as Los Angeles constantly reinvents itself.

Fleishmann, had hauled an old louver press back from California so in one stop a guy could get a beautifully punched, repainted, and pinstriped hood, fender skirts—or whatever.

The business began in the back of a gas station, but soon there were so many cars around that bigger quarters became necessary. H & H Auto Body in Rockville Center, New York, became the new home and one of the owners was kind enough to show Andy how to wield a spray gun just in time to capitalize on the trend toward scalloping and wild paint designs.

Andy's "California Style Striping" became very well known in the East, and examples of his work and some how-to's were featured in the pocket-size Eastern magazines of the day such as *Custom Rodder* and *Car Speed and Style*. Another publication's staff member asked Andy if he had any pictures from California and the next thing he knew, the roadster and the '56 were adorning a 1957 *Rodding and Restyling* cover. Then a story on "Drags at Salinas" was run under Andy's by-line—and he even got paid. His career as a magazine contributor had begun.

As the striping and scalloping business flourished, Andy got the hots for a '55 Chevy. He immediately added a Duntov cam, which enabled him to hold the Powerglide in low and wind it until the pushrods bent. Neat huh? Some chrome was removed, scallops were applied over the existing metallic bronze, and Andy was again in a distinctive car. Literally, countless scallop, stripe and louver jobs were turned out during these years, earning Andy a pretty decent income; enough so that when the '58 Impala came out he couldn't wait to have one. Of course, after a week or two, Andy became completely bored with a stocker and within a month

Few of my photographs from that first Motorama remain, however, this chopped '49 Chevy Club Coupe owned by Dan Landon and rebuilt by Barris' Kustoms was typical of the times.

Alongside the Chevy was this '42 Ford coupe owned by Jack Brumbach of San Francisco. As was often the case, much of the work, including the top chop (5 inches in front tapering to 7 inches in back), was done at Barris'. In place of the original flathead Ford, there resided a '50 Oldsmobile Rocket V-8 and Hydra-Matic transmission.

42 FORD COUPE

of being driven off the showroom floor, the Impala had been turned into one of the most beautiful of the hundreds that were to be customized.

The bodywork was performed to Andy's specs by Herb Gary (the Barris of the east), Kenny punched the louvers, and of course, Andy finished the job in silver-blue scallops over black paint.

After the car was completed, there was still enough cash on hand for a vacation and what better destination than California? The Impala was packed with luggage and two friends and pointed westward to again enjoy, "The weather, the scenery, the cars and the girls." Beginning to sound familiar isn't it?

During Andy's visit to the west coast, finishing touches were added to the Chevy. Appleton spotlights were installed by George Barris himself, a black and white tuck n' roll job was installed in Tijuana, and chrome reversed wheels were purchased from Don Hentzell of the Western Wheel and Rim Company.

When completed, the Impala was the subject of numerous magazine features, including cover stories; even George Barris photographed it.

For months after his return to New York, Andy couldn't get "The weather, the scenery, the cars, and the girls" of California off his mind, especially with 24 inches of snow on the ground. A year or so later Andy loaded up his brand new pearlescent white T-Bird (good money in striping n' scalloping) and in the dead of winter, again headed west. This time he settled in Salinas.

Ever since Andy saw his first *Hot Rod* Magazine in a 1949 high school history class, he had dreamed someday of working for the magazines as a staff writer and photographer. When he went to the L.A. Roadster Exhibition in 1961, his friendship was renewed with Bill Neumann, who also moved west from New York and became editor of *Rod & Custom*. Bill asked Andy to shoot some northern cars for him and pretty soon his photographs were making it on the cover of *R&C*.

Eventually a full time job opened up but 17-hour days combined with a family illness regrettably caused a move back to Salinas, where Andy has lived ever since.

Sadly, the Flying "A" station is gone, as is Sal's, Shelton's, Foster Freeze, and of course Mel's—replaced by a Burger King. And, as Andy and I sat down to write this book in July 1992, the City Council of Salinas, California, banned the decades-old tradition of cruising as had the city of Modesto before it.

Hopefully, however, the good memories of those halcyon days live on in the pages of this book.

Tony Thacker
Huntington Beach, California

By the looks of my haircut, I was home on leave from the Army when this photograph was taken of my '49 Ford parked alongside Johnny Clegg's '32 coupe and Fritz Doering's '49 Merc.

Custom Cars of the Fifties

Previous pages

After getting out of the Army I bought a brand new '55 T-Bird and drove out to California to go to Brook's Institute. Because of the waiting list to get into the school, I drove up to Salinas to see my old friend Willie Wilde, who operated Wilde's Custom Shop of Gonzales, California. Willie's car was the '40 Ford DeLuxe coupe.

The first car show I attended after moving to Salinas in July 1955 was the Motorama held as usual at the Pan-Pacific Auditorium in Los Angeles. Owner-builder George Gowland chopped this '51 Crestline 7 1/2 inches to display the prowess of his Desert Hot Springs shop. Upholstered at Gaylord's, it featured two '50 Merc grille shells and nine bars from a '55 DeSoto grille.

Right

Also at the Motorama was this satin-gold 1950 Olds 98 owned by Robbie Martinez of Chula Vista, California, where he operated the Broadway Auto Body Shop. The stretched-out appearance was attributed to the '55 Cad headlights and '55 Packard taillights. A three-piece '55 Pontiac bumper was installed with exhaust tips exiting from each corner.

Top and left

This chopped '50 Ford convertible was built by Don Holt and Dick Meeks. Note the red and white plastic dash knobs originally designed by Bob Hirohata and sold to the Cal Custom accessory company.

Above

Until the advent of the first true postwar cars, the '41 Ford was popular with customizers, the '40 being difficult to update without major alterations. That fact notwithstanding, Barris Kustoms discarded all four fenders of Frank Monteleon's '41 convertible and replaced them with those from a '50 Olds. Of course, the new fenders didn't match the '41's slabsided doors, so the fender lines were extended with rolled sheet metal incorporating functional scoops. The grille floats within a '50 Merc shell. Even the outer edges of the hood were swiped from a Cadillac. Seven years of extensive work culminated in a pink and white Gaylord interior, with over 500 1-inch pleats, a removable steel top made from the turret of a '38 sedan, and a three-tone paint job.

This gray and black '51 Merc was photographed in 1955 at the Los Angeles Pan-Pacific Motorama. The car features a '53 Olds grille insert, louvered hood, and a radical chop job.

One of my favorite customs of the time was Dave Burgarin's '51 Mercury from San Pedro, California. Apparently Dave did his car this way after being hypnotized by the popular Bob Hirohata Merc, which he had seen the previous year at the Pan-Pacific. Dave had Barris do all the work: chopping, '54 Packard taillights, '54 Buick side trim, frenched '53 Buick headlight doors, and a '52 Chrysler front bumper. Incidentally, George Barris drove that motorized quarter midget into a fence at the Monterey Kap Kapades and badly damaged it.

While not the most popular vehicle to modify, this '54 Mercury nevetheless received a severe chop.

Frank Livingston, then a member of Satan's Angels and still active in the sport today, drove this golden bronze '49 Chevy to the San Jose drag strip. Shankin's Custom Shop of Oakland fitted the hooded '51 Frazer taillights in extended rear fenders and routed exhaust tips through a '51 Pontiac bumper. After removing all the chrome—including the door handles, which were replaced with a push-button system—the car was painted a luminous gold by Pinoli's of San Leandro, California.

Then as now, the annual Oakland Roadster Show was the highlight of the West Coast car show circuit. In February 1956 Gene Winfield showed this chopped, lime-green '51 Merc coupe. At the time, Winfield had his shop in Modesto, California, where he built a string of famous customs.

Seen at the 1956 Oakland show, Johnny Zupan's Merc originally belonged to Louie Bettancourt and was built at Gil Ayala's shop where the top was chopped 3 inches and the body lowered 6 inches by C'ing the frame and stepping the A-arms. The fade-away fenders were also the work of Ayala. However, the car went to Barris', where they did the grille and bumper work and painted it Tingia maroon lacquer. The interior was done by Carson Upholstery Shop.

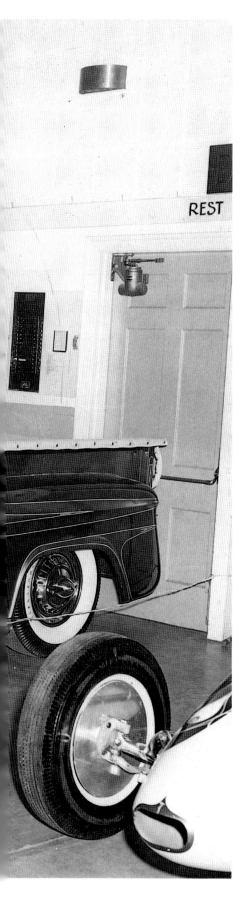

Left

The Wildcat Dream Truck photographed at the 1956 Monterey Kar Kapades. Built by Sam and George, this '54 Ford was owned by Martin and Morris Srabian. It was lowered, featured gold-powdered pearlescent rust metallic lacquer, Dodge hubcaps with spinners made from hand-formed cones, and teeth from a '52 Ford truck grille. Sadly, it burned in the famous Barris' shop fire of 1958.

The northern California show-car circuit included the Monterey Kar Kapades sponsored by the Slo-Pokes Car Club. Originally a racing club—they had the fastest cars around—they put on a popular show that attracted cars from Washington State to Los Angeles, including Johnny Zupan's '49 Merc coupe built at Barris Kustoms. To the left is "Blackie" Gegeian's roadster—America's Most Beautiful Roadster, 1955. That's a clean-shaven Blackie standing off to the left.

Salinas, 1956. My '56 Ford alongside Bob Moore's chopped '51 Merc. Bob still lives in Salinas but I don't know what happened to the car.

Willie Wilde standing proudly beside his chopped '51 Ford Victoria under construction—he never did finish that car but he finished many others. Willie now resides in Florida and at one time managed the Don Garlits Museum of Drag Racing.

Things weren't working out for me in Salinas, so I drove my brand new '56 Ford Victoria back to New York late in 1956. Pinstriped, lowered, nosed, and decked and with a louvered hood (good friend Willie Wilde handled the body work), it was an instant hit in my home town of Oceanside, Long Island, New York. Word got around that I was back in town and had taken up pinstriping, so I was soon contacted by Sam Joosten of *Rodding & Restyling* magazine. Sam had me supply features on both my '56 and my '27 T roadster pickup, which I eventually painted glade green to match the '56. Actually, the T had been sold in Los Angeles before I returned to New York.

Before I went to H & H (Hayden & Hayden), I was striping in a bay at the back of this gas station. Posing along side me and my scalloped and striped '55 Chevy is Jack Schleich the owner of the channeled, metallic green Deuce coupe.

A radical East Coast car of the time was Herb Gary's highly customized '49 Plymouth. Herb was the Barris of the East Coast and his own car featured solid-bar grille, rear fenders extended 13 inches, and a 4 inch section job. The car also employed a hydraulically operated continental kit and trunk lid.

Right

In 1957 I went up to Joe Kizis' Hartford, Connecticut, Motorama where I met Spence Murray and saw the *Rod & Custom* Dream Truck as it was first presented in lavender pearl. With modifications directed by 2,500 reader responses, the "rolling laboratory," as it was termed, took four years and $10,000 to complete visiting in the course of its construction such shops as Davis Custom Shop, Gates Autobody, Valley Custom Shop, and Winfield's Custom before finishing up at Barris'. Sometime after this photograph was taken, the Dream Truck was wrecked in an auto accident on its way to a show back East, however, the truck was to be rebuilt. Little did I know that six years later I would be working with *Rod & Custom* magazine as managing editor. Though I soon left the staff, I continued to contribute as a freelancer up until the 1980s.

ROD and CUSTOM
magazine
DREAM TRUCK
Estimated value $10,000

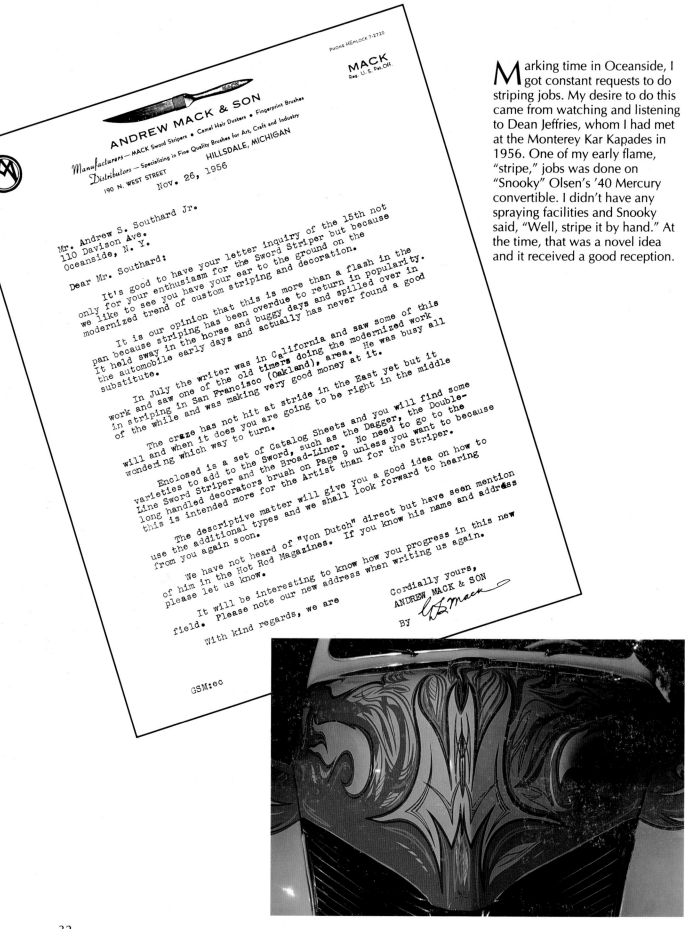

PHONE HEMLOCK 7-2720

MACK
Reg. U.S. Pat. Off.

ANDREW MACK & SON

Manufacturers—MACK Sword Stripers • Camel Hair Dusters • Fingerprint Brushes
Distributors—Specializing in Fine Quality Brushes for Art, Craft and Industry

190 N. WEST STREET   HILLSDALE, MICHIGAN

Nov. 26, 1956

Mr. Andrew S. Southard Jr.
110 Davison Ave.
Oceanside, N. Y.

Dear Mr. Southard:

It's good to have your letter inquiry of the 15th not
only for your enthusiasm for the Sword Striper but because
we like to see you have your ear to the ground on the
modernized trend of custom striping and decoration.

It is our opinion that this is more than a flash in the
pan because striping has been overdue to return in popularity.
It held sway in the horse and buggy days and spilled over in
the automobile early days and actually has never found a good
substitute.

In July the writer was in California and saw some of this
work and saw one of the old timers doing the modernized work
in striping in San Francisco (Oakland), area. He was busy all
of the while and was making very good money at it.

The craze has not hit at stride in the East yet but it
will and when it does you are going to be right in the middle
wondering which way to turn.

Enclosed is a set of Catalog Sheets and you will find some
varieties to add to the Sword, such as the Dagger, the Double-
Line Sword Striper and the Broad-Liner. No need to go to the
long handled decorators brush on Page 9 unless you want to because
this is intended more for the Artist than for the Striper.

The descriptive matter will give you a good idea on how to
use the additional types and we shall look forward to hearing
from you again soon.

We have not heard of "Von Dutch" direct but have seen mention
of him in the Hot Rod Magazines. If you know his name and address
please let us know.

It will be interesting to know how you progress in this new
field. Please note our new address when writing us again.

With kind regards, we are

Cordially yours,
ANDREW MACK & SON

By G.S. Mack

GSM:ec

Marking time in Oceanside, I got constant requests to do striping jobs. My desire to do this came from watching and listening to Dean Jeffries, whom I had met at the Monterey Kar Kapades in 1956. One of my early flame, "stripe," jobs was done on "Snooky" Olsen's '40 Mercury convertible. I didn't have any spraying facilities and Snooky said, "Well, stripe it by hand." At the time, that was a novel idea and it received a good reception.

Monster shirts were popular at the time—the mid- and late-fifties. Dean Jeffries of Los Angeles did this shirt for my buddy, Ken Fleischman. This photograph was taken at one of the small car shows held at Rupp Chevrolet in Lynbrook, New York.

One of the dozens of customs which came under my brush was this '53 Mercury. I did so many I don't even remember the owners' names. A neat touch was the mini flames on the front edge of the fender skirts. And, true to form at the time, continental kits were prevalent on East Coast cars.

Yet another of my striping jobs adorned this '51 Mercury. Again, I don't know the owner's name.

Overloaded with "home" work, I started to do work at H & H (Hayden & Hayden) Auto Body in Rockville Center, Long Island. H & H did the bodywork, and Ken Fleischman, a close friend of mine, punched louvers with a "Verne Lacey," Salinas, California-made press which Ken had dragged back to New York. I handled the pinstriping and scalloping. There was plenty of work and I acquired a brand new '58 Impala. It had but a couple hundred miles on it when I took it to Herb Gary, who changed the front end to my design, fitted a floating-bar grille, filled all the body seams, removed the chrome, including the door handles, and reworked the taillights to match the grille. Herb also fitted a screw jack into the trunk.

Right

Herb applied the black lacquer and the candy silver blue scallops while I applied the finishing stripes. Though I never wanted a black car I knew the quality of Gary's black paint jobs would make it acceptable to me. The chrome reverse wheels were bought through Western Wheel and Rim Co., operated by Don Hentzell who in later years became a fellow Bay Area Roadster Club member with me. Sadly, Don has since passed away. He was a great friend.

Guys in California were going over the border to TJ [Tijuana] to get their upholstery done. There, a full interior cost less than half the US price but some guys preferred to take their own thread—the Mexican thread supposedly being weaker. I never had any problems, though. I drove out in July 1958 and while we enjoyed the sights of TJ, not straying too far from the car, we waited a scant nine hours while they put in a new headliner and installed pleated inserts in the seats and door panels.

This comparison shot shows my completed '58 with that of Bob Boerckel. Bob was another Long Island guy whose car was fitted with one of the popular Cal Custom tube grille kits. When photographing Bob's car and girlfriend, I tried to recreate that "California-look" depicted in the magazines of the owner and their girlfriend—a trend started by George Barris.

WE HAVE A LIMITED SUPPLY OF THOSE POPULAR TEARDROP SPOTLIGHTS!

- 5" SEALED BEAM LENS!
- JEWELER'S CHROME FINISH!
- FULLY ADJUSTABLE— 360° TURNING RADIUS!
- COMPLETE WITH MOUNTING BRACKETS!

Eastern Auto scoops the industry by bringing back the most popular spotlight of all time with custom enthusiasts!

We now have an exclusive supply of luxury-brand lights, designed to our own bullet-shaped specifications, that are the answer to every customizer's dream!

George Barris, famous custom designer and builder, not only endorses these Teardrops—he's installing them on his own custom dream-cars.

Mounts on windshield molding of cars with wrap-around windshields!

Specify make and year of car

HURRY! WHILE THEY LAST $22.50 each

California ROCKET-LITES

For all '52-56 Fords and Thunderbirds. Genuine Olds "Rocket" lenses mounted on sparkling chrome, solid 1-piece rims (no screws or rivets). Simple conversion in minutes—no cutting, welding, or drilling.

Only $11.95 per set

California WHEEL BULLETS

Newest hubcap sensation: for example, see the new Thunderbird for '57! Now—get the same results by customizing your present hubcaps with these brand new conversion spinners, and save $18! Flashing, bullet-shaped chrome spinners—bolt on any hubcap in seconds!

Only $7.95 per set!

FLIPPER BLADES can be attached in any combination (3, 4 or more); are available at just 69¢ each!

PUSH-BUTTON WINDOW LIFTS

Genuine TRICO units for 2 windows. Lifts, switches, all parts. Ford '35-55; Merc. '39-55 (Specify) $19.95 set

Eastern Auto
389 C2 20. GRAND AVE.
LOS ANGELES, CALIFORNIA

25% Deposit Required, F.O.B. Los Angeles, Postage C.O.D. Add 4% Sales Tax in California.

Though this Eastern Auto ad was published in 1957, before Eastern moved to Western Avenue, it was the only one we could find that depicted the teardrop spotlights. Pity you can't find them these days for $22.50.

Back in Los Angeles, I went to Eastern Auto on Western Avenue, where I purchased a pair of original Appleton spotlights. The salesman there said, "Barris installs our spotlights, he has the long bit necessary."

42

I'd intended to go to Barris' anyway, so I drove straight from Eastern Auto to Barris' shop on Atlantic Boulevard. Note that the shop underwent a facelift since my first visit in 1952. While I looked on in fear of that long drill bit cracking my windshield, George quipped, "I haven't cracked many." With the spots installed, George suggested my car was so nice he'd like to shoot a feature, so we drove over to the famous Lynwood City Hall parking lot. The ensuing feature appeared in *Motor Life* magazine.

Right
*A*ndy Southard and his works *were featured on dozens of magazine covers, including these two* Car Speed & Style *covers. That's one of Andy's paint jobs on the cover on the left, and Andy himself at work on the cover on the right.*

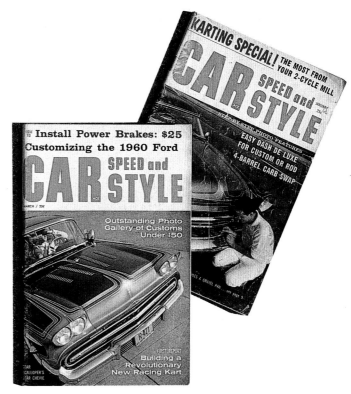

Left

Barris was always looking for a way to turn a buck and in the December 1959 issue of *Rod & Custom* magazine ran this ad for glossy prints of some of the shop's more famous creations. What we'd give for a set of those prints now.

Looking at my car parked in the back of Barris' shop is Larry Watson (left) and Eddie Rhodes, a Bellflower High School buddy of Watson's. Larry acquired fame as a painter and pinstriper and eventually went on to do some motion picture and TV work. The car to the left of mine was Junior Conway's '50 Ford coupe. Junior is credited with having the first chopped '41 Merc with full fadeaways.

Having had a '49 coupe like
Junior's, I've always admired
his car. Standing alongside me is
my fellow New York buddy "Izzy"
Davidson. Behind us is a burnt-out
roadster lost in the fire of '58.

Famous customizer Bill Hines had recently moved out from Detroit and started working for Barris and here's a rear shot of his '51 Ford business coupe, which he called "Lil' Bat." Chopped 4 inches, it featured wild fabricated rear fenders and taillights from a '56 Ford. The lengthened rear bumper is adorned with a Kaiser centerpiece. Radiused wheel openings displayed Caddy "sombrero" hubcaps. Gold scalloping was added sometime after this picture was taken. Ahead of Bill's Bat is Dean Jeffries' Porsche 356 coupe. To the left is Jayne Mansfield's Lincoln, which, I remember, had a mink interior, which had a foul odor.

B arris' famous Ala Kart, two-time winner of "America's Most Beautiful Roadster" and owned by Dick Peters, was undergoing some minor work before being trailered to the Long Beach Show in this July 1958 shot. Behind the Kart can be seen the charred remains of a Deuce roadster destroyed in the shop fire of '58. In all, fourteen vehicles were destroyed in that fire including Jayne Mansfield's Jaguar, the president of Richfield Oil Company's limousine, and the Wildcat pickup. According to Barris, Dean Jeffries saw the fire from across the street, ran over and opened the door sucking the fire from the front to the rear of the shop. Archie Moore's magnesium car really helped the flames but Jeff got in his girlfriend's '56 Chevy and backed it out just in time. The fire stopped right at the Ala Kart....

Not all customs are for show only. Bill Carr's '55 Chevy "Aztec" was driven regularly and here it is parked on the street in front of Barris' shop. Bill also worked at Barris' and no doubt the car was pulled inside for some detailing before going to the show. The Aztec sported a 3/4-race Corvette engine and an overall height of just 48 inches achieved with a front spindle kit, de-arched springs, lowering blocks and a C'd frame. The top was chopped 3 1/2 inches and the fins were extended 18 inches. The car was painted with thirty coats of Golden Honey lacquer and the interior sported the standard show car pleats a-plenty.

Left

A young Dean Jeffries can be seen here pinstriping the edges of a flamed '57 Chevy trunk lid.

What a picture—Larry Watson, Dean Jeffries, and Eddie Rhodes in the same place, Barris' shop, at the same time, July 1958. As you can see, the distinctive copper-plated grille made from '57 Mercury bumpers is missing from the Kopper Kart.

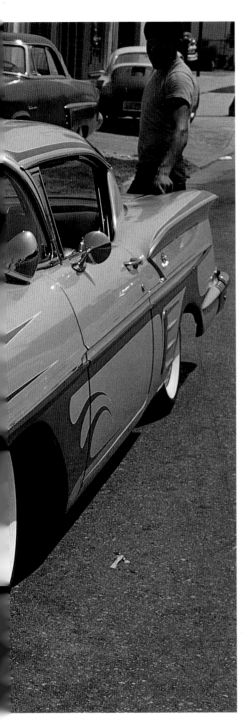

A typical street car of the era was this lowered '58 Chevy with Cal Custom grille and a scallop job—the chrome wasn't even removed. The guy was at Barris' to get a quote for repainting after his car had been maliciously damaged with a "church key."

Spotted on a used car lot in Burbank was this much modified '57 T-Bird owned by Dick Jackson. Dick built this car while working at Barris'. Vertical bar grille was gold-color chromed to match the Jeffries' scalloping. Note also the Buick fender portholes in the hood and the pleated top.

Parked on the street in Long
Beach, this candy red Chevy
looked good so I had to
photograph it.

Before there was ever a Roth Studios there was Barron, Roth and Kelly, where on Atlantic Boulevard the threesome performed miracles of pinstriping, flames, and scallops. And, if you look closely at the guy with no shirt standing next to the '58 Chevy, as Honest Charley would say, "It's Ed Roth hisself."

After a while this camper pulled in and almost before I could get my camera going, Kelly, a "lefty," had lettered "Bellflower, California" on the back. As you can see, Kelly's purple Chevy sported the era's most stolen hubcap, that of the Olds Fiesta. (When we went to the movies, we'd pop our hubcaps in the trunk. It got so bad we'd even remove the dummy spots and lock those in the car also.) The Chevy also sported a logo, "Sno Go," which was a popular adornment of the period.

Another view of Barron, Roth and Kelly shows another fastback Chevy and a chopped '32 Ford pickup with color-chromed "baldy" hubcaps—another period trend.

Left

The word flames says everything about Ed Roth's Bel Air hardtop sporting Lincoln hubcaps with color-chromed purple centers. Another trendy thing at the time was the use of chrome tape to stripe the roof.

Another product from the Barris shop was Hersh "Junior" Conway's '50 Ford, photographed at the Gardena outdoor car show. The car, a favorite of mine, featured numerous mods including blended '51 Mercury grille sections and floating-bar grille, shaded '55 Chevy headlights, peaked hood with scoops, filled bumper with '53 Mercury bumper guards, V'd windshield sealed with clear plastic cement, and '55 Buick taillights. The clever combo of side trim, dividing two-tone bronze paint, is from a '53 Dodge and '55 Ford. Skirts are from a '57 Merc.

After leaving Barron, Roth and Kelly's, we spotted fellow customizer Gary Simpson of Long Beach, California, driving his '58 Buick Special hardtop. Body mods were minor but original. For example, check out those '56 Buick portholes sunk into the tops of each fender, '58 Edsel hubcaps, and popular full-length "cut-out" side exhausts. Again, the top features single-toned stripes.

The scallop craze went unchecked as this Renault 4CV shot on the street shows. The owner of the Plymouth in the background who'd stopped to look, was equally intrigued.

Photographed on the streets of
San Diego in July 1958, a
chopped and scalloped Chevy.

Duane Stek's "Moonglow" has always been a role model for chopped '54 Chevys. Featuring '56 Chrysler taillights, hubcaps with added Olds "flipper bars," '54 Chevy grille with an additional ten Chevy grille bars, frenched '52 Ford headlights, and '56 Chevy rear bumper, it had a 3 1/2-inch top chop with a Plexiglass rear window. The powder blue and white upholstery was stitched by Del's Trim Shop and a young Larry Watson was responsible for the paint and striping.

Right
The reincarnated *Rod & Custom* Dream Truck. For a while, after it was repaired, it was painted pearl white and fitted with a radically restyled bed by Robert Metz of Indiana, then it was painted green as it appeared here in the Long Beach show in 1958. Today, in the hands of current owner Kurt McCormick, it is once again pearl white. In the background is Ala Kart and Junior's Ford.

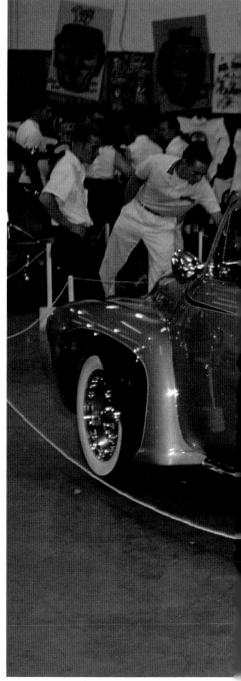

AUTHORIZED
PERSONNEL
Only

G 35 216

THE ROD & CUSTOM MAGAZINE *Dream Truck*

Harold Johnson's pearl white lacquered '51 Chevy had frenched headlights, filled seams, a Merc grille shell with floating bar, louvered hood, and green scallops painted by Larry Watson.

Titled "Violet Fade," the paint on Lanny Erickson's '56 Chevy chopped two-door sedan had to be seen to be believed. The bodywork included: '54 Chevy straight-bar grille assembly floating in a stock opening, nosed, peaked, and louvered hood, popular chrome-reverse wheels with homemade hubcaps and accessory spinners. The lower chrome trim came from a '57 DeSoto, and the taillight lenses are from a '56 Lincoln . And look how low that car is as I raise my arm over the top to show the boys back home.

Selected by Trend Books' (Petersen) *Custom Cars* as one of "The 10 Best" of 1959, Larry Watson's '58 T-Bird utilized a special formula paint developed by Joe Sheline of Long Beach, California, resulting in a deep tone of transparent burgundy lacquer topped with silver pearl scallops. Incidentally, Larry customized this car only three weeks after buying it brand new, the extensive body mods being performed at Barris Kustoms. I'm still in touch with Larry and we've been friends all these years.

Right
Joe Bailon-built '56 Chevy convertible sporting a candy-apple red and gold paint job. Note the rare Satan's Angels club plaque.

Left

Early in 1956, *Car Craft* commissioned illustrator Don Fell to restyle the '49-'52 Chevy with the idea of having the leading shops of the era carry out the work on this "guinea pig stovebolt." The car went through many shops, including Valley Custom, Norm's Auto Body, Barris', and George Cerny's before turning up on this car lot in Burbank—what a bargain at $1,095. The transformation was accomplished by altering only four components along with minor trim removal, and the price tag was held well beneath the $1,000 mark. The mods included a dechromed and peaked hood, '55 Olds headlight rims, a '55 Chevy grille, and 8-inch fender extensions housing '55 Plymouth taillights.

Though I never found out who owned this '57 Ford photographed on the street in Monterey, the modifications were performed by Dick Archibald while Paul Vona painted it. It was a nice street car of its time.

The seldom-restyled '48 Chevy got the full treatment from Tony Cardoza of Pacific Grove, California. Tony, a member of the Aristocrats, fitted Chrysler Windsor grille bars into a one-piece-molded and reshaped shell, filled and fitted scoops in the hood, and frenched '53 Ford headlights with quarter-moon air scoops underneath while Moon caps, side exhausts, and pushbutton doors add to the smooth appearance. Tony designed all of the mods and did most of the work himself, the other work being carried out by Foriegion's Auto Body Shop in Monterey, California.

A typical local-to-Salinas car was this lowered, nosed, and decked '56 Chevy hardtop belonging to Greg Sargenti, a schoolmate of customizer Rod Powell. Incidentally, the car was painted and striped by Don Varner as well.

Following pages
A local car painted by famous customizer Don Varner was this '56 Ford owned by Hugh England. Sadly, that Mobil gas station is long gone.

Back in New York, I was as busy as ever now doing full paint jobs as well as striping and scalloping. This '57 Chevy two-door, the first of the 270 horsepower models, belonged to Al Carreno, a good friend at the time. Al was a racer, the car was a stick-shift goer, and for a time there I got mixed up with the local racers. Basically, Al's car had a louvered hood and one of my "conservative" scallop jobs.

Corvettes were popular cars to customize and I did my share, this particular one belonging to Steve Diskin of Long Beach, New York. The base color was charcoal and I scalloped it in candy red with white striping.

I painted Frank Tromboli's '58 Chevy Bel Air in September 1958. Again, it was nosed and decked and had a louvered hood with a Cal Custom grille.

Late in October 1958 I went to the Teaneck, New Jersey, car show where I photographed this '55 Ford fitted with '56 Olds headlight rims and a '56 Canadian Meteor grille—an unusual modification. The rear end featured '56 Merc station wagon lamps in peaked rear fenders.

For a job like this '52 Ford I would have probably charged $75 for a straight scallop and stripe. Bigger and wilder jobs ran about $150 to $200. And the average job like this took three days to tape, sand, paper it off, spray it, and stripe it. If there was time, I'd take a photograph. Also I'd try to fit in small stripe jobs between the bigger jobs. The average stripe job was $25, so if I could squeeze in two or three a day, I'd be looking good.

As you can see, this '50 Ford coupe has been chopped and made into a hardtop by removing the post. Back then that was a very unusual modification but nevertheless effective.

Right
In July 1959 *Car Craft* voted San Franciscan Jerry Anolik's '55 T-Bird Oakland's "most bizarre exhibit." Seen here in Teaneck, Jerry's bird of a different feather featured quad Lucas lamps in a front end redesigned because of an earlier crash. The engine was a blown Caddy.

There weren't too many chopped '58 Chevys around when this one turned up in Teaneck. Built at Barris', the "Kandy Kart" featured an unusual padded top, '59 Cad taillights, louvered hood, molded side scoops, and candy paint.

Ken was still punching louvers
and I was still striping. And
don't you just love that interior?

Ed Hayden of H & H bought this '56 Ford convertible as a present for his wife. Ed nosed and decked it and fitted some different taillights before we both painted it candy red, after which I painted the scallops and striped it. Ed's wife was totally surprised, and pleased.

Another growing trend of the time was to punch louvers in Moon-style hubcaps after which I striped them. This particular customer wanted them black with gold hearts but the combinations were limitless.

One of the nicer cars that came out of Brooklyn was Bob Carducci's '48 Chevy convertible known as the "Fabian Continental." Powered then by a '56 Chevy V-8, trans, and rear end, it featured a '50 Merc shell housing a '53 Chevy grille, '55 Pontiac bumpers, Caddy headlights, and extended rear fenders adapted from a '55 Pontiac with Chevy taillights. Much of the work was done by the Cove Custom Shop in Hillside, New Jersey. However, I added the scallops and stripes in April 1959 and shot these photographs just as the sun was going down.

Sunset shots were often all I could get because I'd get the job finished toward the end of the day and the owner would be impatient to take his car away. For example, this '58 Ford was sitting outside the shop and all I got were a few shots.

There are a lot more mods than meet the eye in Ron Fagundes' chopped '52 Ford Victoria featured on the April 1959 cover of *Custom Rodder*. The biggest change resulted from the grafting, by Barris, of a complete '54 Merc top chopped 5 inches. Barris also adapted the '54 Dodge rear window and extended the trunk 6 inches between rear glass and deck lid. Ron tried his own hand at customizing with a '54 Pontiac grille bar. Tunneled headlights, '58 Impala side trim, scoops, and electronic door latches more or less completed the metalwork before Vallejo's A-1 Body Works applied the paint. Transferred to Mitchell Field Base on Long Island, Ron had me apply the lime gold scallops and stripes, proving that east meets west even in the custom car scene of 1958.

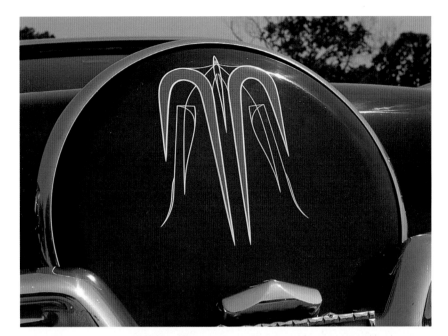

Another nice street custom which never made it between the covers of a magazine was this '57 Ford that I scalloped and striped. Though personally never particularly fond of the East Coast trend for continental kits, I was very pleased with my work on this one.

Another one I know nothing about is this '58 Chevy convertible, which featured dual mirrors and dual antennas. Though I didn't paint the car, I did scallop and stripe it.

Few contemporary magazines had the color availability to show color photographs of actual work in progress, the color being reserved for the front cover. These two photographs I took by setting up my camera on a tripod and using my self timer and shooting a flash picture. I did this because I wanted a picture of myself spraying and being that it was a hot August night, I had to take my shirt off. Back then we didn't have face masks, let alone a spray booth. The car was a '56 Ford four-door sedan owned by Ray and Jo Milazzo. Today Ray Milazzo, whom I'm still in touch with, is a member of the Los Angeles Roadster Club, owning a '32 Ford Cabriolet. Notice the difference in dress when I got to the striping part.

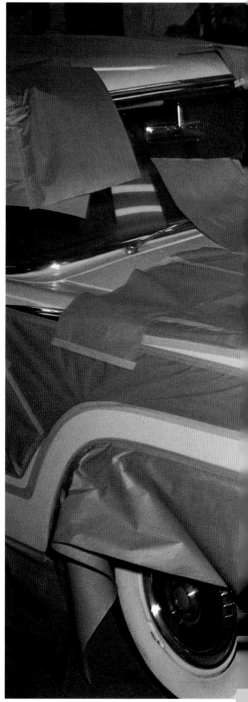

Joe Bailon was credited with the bodywork on Frank Caraway's '58 Chevy Impala "Scoopee Doo." Supposedly, the first time around, when the car was cotton candy pink, it had thirty air scoops fore and aft. Frank delivered the car and said, "Go the route." Obviously Joe didn't go far enough and over the winter of 1959 the car was completely redone, being channeled 4 inches and having the front and rear ends extensively reworked before Joe repainted it candy red. You can see that just about this time the show cars were beginning to get rather radical. Incidentally, Bailon was noted for his tubular bumpers and the trend for exhausts exiting through the body was also getting popular.

In attendance at the 1960 San Jose show was the man hisself, a young Joe Bailon seen here on the left behind that candy red '59 Chevy. Normally I wouldn't intrude and take people's photographs, preferring to take candid shots of them in the background.

An extremely clean '50 Merc convertible was this pearl white example shown by Lloyd Meyers a member of the Rod Wheelers car club of San Jose, California—a big club at the time. Car had chopped top, tube grille, '57 Lincoln quad headlights, and DeSoto trim separating the paint scheme.

R on Aguirre's much modified
'56 Corvette featured quad
lights, new grille assembly and
shell, exaggerated fins, and wild
pearl paint.

NO. 147
CLASS: CUSTOM HARDTOP
OWNER: GEORG DIAS

SAN JUAN BAUTISTA
53 CHEVY
ENG. 58 CHEVY V8 181¾

Left
Another example of the craze for stacked quad headlights was George Dias' '53 Chevy seen here at San Jose with tube bumpers, fade paint, and chrome-reverse rims.

Custom Plymouths were not that popular but Louie Stojanovich's Chrysler-powered '48 was a peach. It was later reworked by Winfield's Custom Shop and painted candy tangerine at Barris'.

At the 1960 Sacramento show, Jim Skonzakes from Dayton, Ohio, showed the Barris-built "Golden Sahara II." The cost at the time of its original construction was said to be $25,000, and that was before the front end was completely redone. Subsequently, back in Dayton, complete electronic controls allowing remote-control operation were added. Much of the trim was gold plated and the paint was oriental pearl. Inside, the Sahara featured a TV, tape recorder, telephone, and a bar with a built-in refrigerator. According to George Barris, the Sahara started life as his personal Lincoln. He'd only owned it thirty days but crashed it in the fog towing Dan Rather's '49 Chevy back from the Sacramento show in '53 or '54.

This picture was taken at the 1960 Oakland Roadster Show and depicts E. J. Wilhelm standing alongside his highly customized '36 Ford "Mark Mist." Though originally owned by Richie Feliz, Wilhelm eventually bought the car, made some changes, and did well at the shows. "Mark Mist" portrayed all of the popular trends of the time and then some. Today, Wilhelm is retired but still manages some work in his San Jose garage.

Jerry Sahagon, who operated an upholstery shop next to Joe Bailon's old shop in Hayward, California, owned this chopped '51 Chevy coupe. Reworked by Bailon, it sported a grille made from two '54 Buick bumpers, round rod center bars, and seven '53 Merc teeth. The rear end treatment is pretty wild too and it features a typical Bailon candy apple paint job.

Right
Don Tognotti, current promoter of the Oakland Roadster Show, displayed his "Green Voodoo" '55 Thunderbird at the Sacramento show in February 1960. Restyled by Ricky's Custom Shop, it featured quad headlights, tube grille, and split bumpers from a '55 Pontiac.

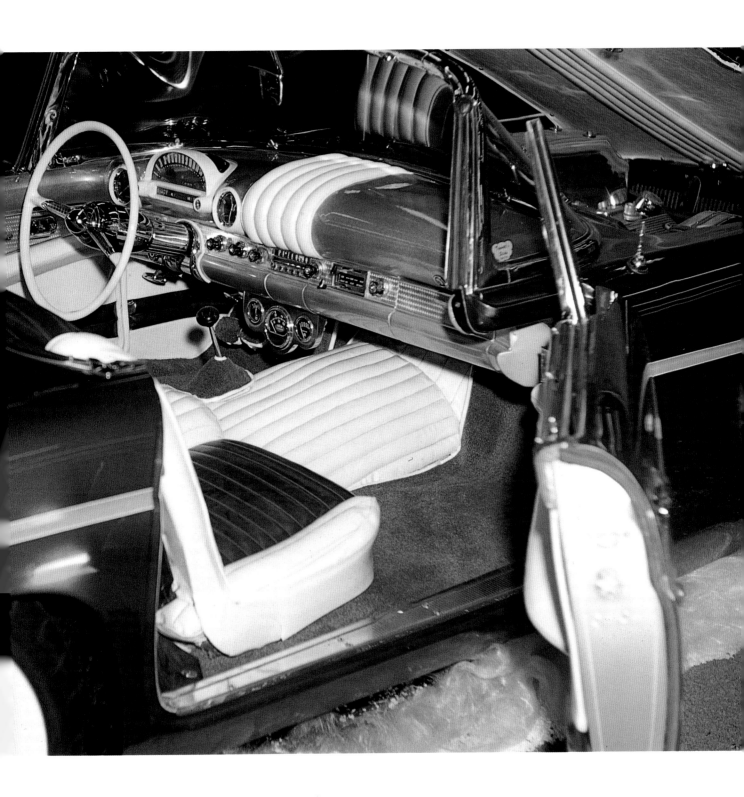

Sacramento, 1960. D. McCutcheon's '55 Buick "Kandy Kane" with a claimed value of $4,500. The paint was by Larry Watson and the upholstery was by Gooch in Mexico.

S am Barris eventually opened up
his own shop, for a short period
of time, in Carmichael, California,
where he customized "El
Capitola," Don Fletcher's '57
Chevy photographed here at
Sacramento early in 1960. It was
the only time I ever saw the car.
While Sam handled the extensive
modifications, which included 3
1/2-inch chop, twin Lucas lights,
an extensively reworked grille
with split '57 DeSoto bumpers,
and side trim from both a '54
Pontiac and '53 Olds with
extruded aluminum inserts,
brother George's shop in Lynwood
handled the paint. I have no idea
what happened to this car.

An extremely rare car to come under the customizer's torch was the '48 Studebaker, especially a four-door. Nevertheless, Barris Kustoms attacked the "Modern Grecian" with gusto, sectioning the body 5 inches and chopping the top 4 inches. The V-shaped rear fenders were constructed of tubing paneled with extruded aluminum while the taillights were handmade of red plastic with frosted cross sections. Frosted plastic was also used to cover the frenched headlights. The paint was pearlized lime gold with green diamond-dust panels. The impressive interior, with four-way swivel bucket seats was upholstered by Eddie Martinez. Note the aircraft-style steering wheel.

Another clean car appearing at the San Jose show was this '56 Chevy belonging to John Moskito. Notice how in those days the show cars were jammed tightly together. Notice also the advent of "Angel Hair" as the display became as important as the vehicle.

During one of my many trips to Hollywood I stopped in to see Dean Jeffries, who had set up his own shop after leaving Barris'. When I arrived he was about to spray this Ferrari and I said, "Do you mind if I stay and shoot a few photographs?" Jeff has always been very accommodating and I hung around taking photographs while he laid down a real "wet" candy job. Notice again the lack of any protection.

Parked right across the street from Jeffries' shop was this '56 Ford F-100 owned by Johnny Zupan from Denver, Colorado. I believe Jeff used to use this as a shop truck. Built by Barris Kustoms, it had a rolled front pan, quad lights, and the center grille piece from a '57 Chevy. It also had chrome running boards and twin exhausts running along the edge of the pickup bed—a popular truck fad. The paint, by Jeff, was Lime Gold and Organic Green. The spinner bars on the Olds Fiesta hubcaps were gold plated.

Right
In the June 1960 issue of *Car Craft* magazine Dean Jeffries ran this ad for his line of crazy stuff. A pair of those sun-visor shades complete with case would be useful even today.

64

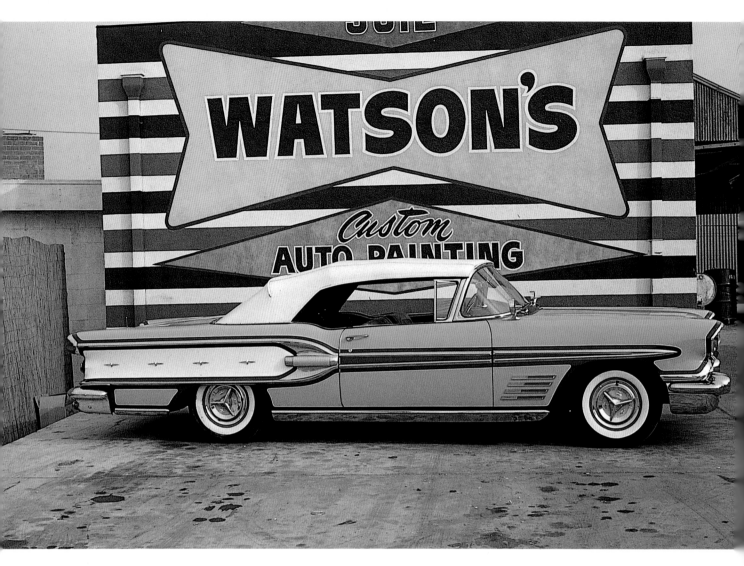

Larry Watson had also ventured out on his own and opened up shop in Bellflower, California, where I took these photographs in March 1960, with Watson's sign making a perfect backdrop for this '58 Pontiac convertible.

Upper right

Larry Watson stands proudly alongside his own '59 Cad with candy burgundy and silver top—a popular treatment.

Lower right

Another car at Watson's that day was this '58 Chevy. Note the use of '59 Caddy taillight lenses. Though each of these cars is conservative, Watson was equally capable of radical work.

B arris Kustom City, redone once
again and photographed in
January 1960. Today, this site is a
muffler shop.

Right
F or once on the other side of the
camera, a young George Barris
poses beside his '59 Caddy.

Two months later I was back at Barris', where the "Kopper Kart" was being cleaned up and prepared to be picked up by its new owner, Jim Skonzakes, owner of the "Golden Sahara." At the time, I wondered if I would ever see the pickup again, so I quickly took this photograph. How lucky I was to be once again in the right place at the right time. The truck has not been seen or heard of in many years. Apparently, its new owner chopped it up and left it sitting in his garage.

Right

A rare photograph of the front of Bill Cushenberry's shop in Seaside, California. Seen working there is Bill (to the right in white coveralls) and to the left Donny Baker, a friend of Bill's.

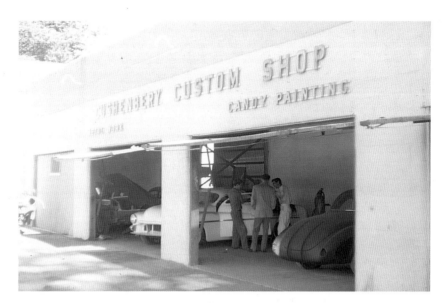

Below

Here's Bill Cushenberry doing lead work on the door of a chopped '51 Merc.

The tail end of the "El Matador," one of Cushenberry's most famous show cars. Notice here the car is still unchopped and that Bill was contemplating a green color. Bill liked green but was eventually talked into painting the car candy red.

"El Matador" made its debut at Harry Costa's San Mateo show—red, not green—where Bill was awarded "People's Choice." El Matador now sported a 4 1/2-inch top chop as well as a 5-inch section. The frame was Z'd and the spring eyes were reversed for maximum lowering. Canted, quad Lucas lights frame a grille that features small plastic tubes. The white pearl Naugahyde interior was done by Bill Manger of Manger's Custom Upholstery of Castroville, California. Bill handled many of the top show cars of the era including: The *Car Craft* "Dream Rod," Cushenberry's "Silhouette," and Gene Boucher's sectioned '56 Ford. Bill is still in business today in Castroville, California.

In February 1960, at picturesque El Estaro Lake, Monterey, California, Bill Cushenberry was gracious enough to park his personal candy red '57 Olds for me to photograph. Don Varner, I believe, did the scallops and striping. Again, not a very radical car but it was very clean being lowered and having shaved door handles.

Left

Later that year, in December, I applied some orange hazing and white pinstriping to the newly painted black Ranchero. The truck was a common sight on the streets of Salinas, I even have some great movie footage of this truck.

Below

Originally owned by Rich Tiago of Hayward, California, and built and painted candy green and gold by Ortez, was this '57 Ford Ranchero called "Outer Space." A severe crash instigated this radical rebuild, which I photographed in February of 1960 when Dick Shirk of Salinas, California, owned it.

Another local-to-Salinas car was this 1951 Ford belonging to Bernard Malbas. This unusual four-door had the rear door handles removed and note how he's painted checkers in the back of the Olds Fiesta hubcaps. A nice street car in its day.

remont Drag Strip in February 1960, but I have no idea who owned this flamed '55 Buick Special. Note the oil cans in the foreground. While not a big racing fan, I'd go when there was a big meet on and Don Garlits or Don Prudhomme was racing. More often I'd go to the local strip in Salinas which is now torn up like so many strips.

Left

Another local four-door, this time a chopped '57 Chevy hardtop restyled by Willie Wilde for Norman Riparetti of Castroville, California. The car featured canted, quad headlights in extended front fenders, an Olds rear window, roof scoops, and wildly extended rear fenders.

Extremely unusual was Dick Gregg's '50 Ford sedan, chopped and sectioned 5 inches by Gregg into a pickup. A molded '50 Merc shell contained a tubular floating grille, '57 Chevy headlights are frenched, and it's seen here in January 1960 being repaired at Bailon's Custom Shop in Haywood, California. What look like chrome bed rails are in fact exhaust pipes.

Nineteen-year-old Paul Vona from Salinas built his "dream car" using a '50 Olds coupe. Rauch Machine Shop lowered it by C'ing the frame in the rear and stepping the front A-arms. After nosing and decking, Paul radiused the rear wheel arches, reworked the grille, and installed '56 Corvette taillights before he and Al Tompkins painted it in pearlescent purple with scallops and stripes. The car appeared, finished, on the cover of the October 1958 issue of *Custom Rodder*, a back-East magazine. However, as you can see, when I photographed it in February 1960 the car was painted in purple primer—a popular trend at the time.

When Jack Snyder's '56 Chevy first appeared in the magazines it was flamed. When I took this photograph in August 1960 it had a custom grille, quad headlights, side lakes pipes, custom taillights, and sported a new candy paint job—all the work having been done at Wilhelm's Custom Shop—and that's Jack Snyder sitting in the car.

Left

Also shot in February 1960 is Dennis Gattis' '57 Buick. Lowered, with Olds Fiesta hubcaps, it had sidepipes, was nosed and decked with a louvered hood, and was scalloped and striped by Don Varner. Fashionably, for the time, it had the name "Ace High" behind the door. Today Dennis runs, with his partner, Chuck Wheelus, a '55-'56-'57 Chevy parts house and is a member of the Salinas Valley Chevy Club.

I can't remember in whose shop I shot Dick Gonzales' '55 Studebaker (*Rod & Custom* cover car for December 1959) where it was undergoing some reworking. Previously, Larry Watson had applied the candy yellow over pearl white paint and Wright's of Long Beach had handled the upholstery. A different look was achieved by installing a '54 Chevy grille, '54 Buick side trim, and Chrysler New Yorker wire wheels. Just visible outside the shop you can see the back end of Johnny Zupan's famous chopped Merc built by Barris. For some reason I never did photograph that car in the state it was in.

ROD & Custom

IND

BONNEVILLE and BIG GO RECORDS!

DECEMBER 1959 25c

STUDE for SHOW
see page 20

Among my numerous trips back and forth to New York, I took the time to lower and paint (platinum pearl) my 1960 Thunderbird. It was nosed and decked and had bullet-type grille, Lincoln hubcaps, and dummy Appleton spotlights—the real ones getting hard to find by 1960.

PETERSEN PUBLISHING COMPANY

Andy Southard, Jr.
Managing Editor
Rod & Custom Magazine

5959 HOLLYWOOD BLVD.   LOS ANGELES 28 · HO 6-2111

Index

"Ace High," 125
Acker, Bill, 8
Aguirre, Ron, 97
"Ala Kart," 47, 64
Anolik, Jerry, 82
Ayala, Gil, 23
"Aztec," 48

Bailon, Joe, 68, 94, 95
Barris Kustoms, 19, 43, 48, 53, 60, 68, 106, 109, 112
Barris, George, 12, 20, 24, 25, 40, 43, 44, 47, 100, 112
Barris, Sam, 25, 105
Bettancourt, Louie, 23
Boerchel, Bob, 40
Burgarin, Dave, 20

Caraway, Frank, 94
Cardoza, Tony, 72
Carr, Bill, 48
Carreno, Al, 76
Clegg, Johnny, 8
Conway, Junior, 44, 60
Cushenberry, Bill, 114, 115, 118

Dias, George, 99
"Dream Rod," 116
"Dream Truck," 64

"El Capitola," 105
"El Matador," 115, 116
Erickson, Larry, 67

"Fabian Continental," 87
Fell, Don, 71

Fleischman, Ken, 36
Fugundes, Ron, 89

Gary, Herb, 12, 30, 36
Gegeian, Blackie, 25
"Golden Sahara II," 100, 113
Gonzales, Dick, 126
Gowland, George, 16
"Green Voodoo," 102
Gregg, Dick, 123

Hayden, Ed, 85
Hentzell, Don, 36
Hines, Bill, 46
Hirohata, Bob, 19, 20

Jackson, Dick, 54
Jeffries, Dean, 10, 46, 47, 51, 54, 108, 109
Johnson, Harold, 66
Joosten, Sam, 28

"Kandy Kane," 104
"Kandy Kart," 83
"Kopper Kart," 51, 113

Livingston, Frank, 22

"Mark Mist," 101
Martinez, Robbie, 16
Metz, Robert, 64
Meyers, Lloyd, 96
Milazzo, Ray, 92
"Modern Grecian," 106
"Moonglow," 64
Moore, Bob, 26

Motorama, 20

"Outer Space," 119

Rhodes, Eddie, 44, 51
Roth, Ed, 56, 59

Sahagon, Jerry, 102
Schleich, Jack, 29
"Scoopee Doo," 94
"Silhouette," 116
Simpson, Gary, 61
Skonzakes, Joe, 100, 113
Snyder, Jack, 125
Stek, Duane, 64
Stojanovich, Louie, 99

Tognotti, Don, 102

Varner, Don, 73, 125
"Violet Fade," 67
Vona, Paul, 124

Watson, Larry, 44, 51, 64, 66, 68, 104, 110, 126
Wilde, Willie, 9, 16, 27, 28, 123
Wilhelm, E.J., 101
Winfield, Gene, 22

Zupan, Johnny, 23, 25, 126